How to Get a Flight Attendant Job

ISBN-13: 978-1479130559

ISBN-10: 1479130559

Copyright Notice

HOW TO GET A FLIGHT ATTENDANT JOB

Linda Grapeth

I dedicate this book to every person — who has been lucky enough to have their lives touched by the joy, excitement and sheer buzz of flying...

Contents

- How to Speak About Success
- Employer Information
- Same Employer. Different Job?
- Choosing a Look for Your Résumé
- What Type of Résumé to Write
- 4 Ways to Find a Job
- Getting Your Résumé Out There
- Getting Past the First Selection
- We Are All Different
- Staying Organized
- Writing Your Cover Letter
- Using the Internet to Boost Your Job Success
- Researching Airlines Online
- How to Use Email to Get a Job
- Getting Social to Find a Job
- Preparing for the Interview
- Know What You're Getting Into

How to Get a
Flight Attendant Job

Do you have the ability to communicate with different kinds of people?

Do you see yourself regularly flying on one of the big aircrafts of a well-known airline?

Are you a team player with a positive attitude towards life and other people?

Can you see yourself visiting the world's big cities while getting paid to do so?

If your answer to these questions is yes, then you're a perfect candidate for the position of flight attendant or cabin crew member.

If you dream of becoming a flight attendant, then you need to realise that this is one career that's highly sought after and therefore involves some tough competition.

It is, in fact, among the top ten careers people dream of having.

If you have a natural love for travel, and genuinely care for other people, then being a flight attendant may just be the perfect career for you. Many people say that being a flight attendant isn't actually a career, but a lifestyle.

Few people know that the first-ever stewardess was a nurse employed by United Airlines back in 1930. At that time, the career required a nursing qualification and was considered by many to be a glamorous job, although the main function was to take care of the medical needs of passengers in case the need arises.

Since then, people with this career have been called by a lot of names: flight stewards and stewardesses, air hostesses, flight attendants, cabin attendants, and cabin crew members.

After the licensing of cabin crew in 1998, South African airlines formally changed the term for their flight attendants to cabin crew members.

The licensing process has also changed the image of the career from one of glamour to one of professionalism and competence. Cabin crew members are now viewed as safety officers with the primary role of ensuring the safety of their passengers, crew members, and the aircraft itself.

The good news today is that air travel is increasing, which means there are more opportunities for you to secure the job of your dreams.

Of course, being the perfect candidate doesn't necessarily mean you'll automatically get the job.

It's important for you to be armed with both professional and insider information. Among other things, you need to learn how to fill out an application form properly, how to prepare yourself for assessment centres, and how to pass interviews.

Do Your Research

The first and perhaps most important thing you need to do is acquire plenty of information about the airline industry and the specific airline you plan to apply for work in.

Of course, you'll need to have your priorities in order and filter the information according to your specific needs and life plans.

Conduct a thorough research on your airline of choice as well as other airlines that may provide good employment opportunities.

Did you know that 90% of candidates fail right at the application stage, not because of the huge number of applicants, but because of their own failure to demonstrate to their prospective employer that they have just the right customer service skills to become part of the cabin crew?

Remember that your responses to the questions on the application form need to match the requirements of the role you're applying for.

Regardless of whether you're using an online application form or submitting the form via post, you need to provide responses that are relevant to the position as well as your own experience and circumstances. Towards this end, you may want to link your application to the job by using phrases like "excellent customer service skills" and "team player."

Are You a Team Worker?

Take note that the selection process for cabin crew typically includes an assessment on your team working skills and during these assessments, recruitment staff will gauge if you posses certain qualities they expect from their cabin crew.

Some of these qualities are the ability to work well with other people and provide positive feedback as well as the ability to offer logical solutions to common customer problems.

Naturally, exceptional customer care skills are also vital qualities for cabin crew so you'll also be assessed for this. As cabin crew, you'll be working closely with people you've just met and may even be thrown into an emergency situation with them, so you must have the ability to work with anyone at any time.

Job Tasks

If you're thinking of applying for work as a flight attendant member, then you should first realise that this type of career isn't all fun and games, and the actual work involved may not be as glamorous as you think. A cabin crew member's responsibilities mostly has to do with passenger safety, with the secondary responsibilities involving customer service such as offering food, drinks, and duty-free goods to passengers.

Specifically, these are the responsibilities of a cabin crew member associated with passenger safety:

1. **Safety Briefing** – Cabin crew members are required to attend a safety briefing with aircraft pilots before each flight.

2. **Cabin Baggage Loading** – Cabin crew members check each baggage for size, weight, and potentially dangerous items.

3. **Safety Check** – Cabin crew members make sure all safety devices on the aircraft are in working order before each flight.

4. **Safety Demo** – Cabin crew members perform a safety demonstration a few minutes before takeoff. In case there's a safety video in the aircraft, cabin crew members are tasked to monitor passenger viewing.

5. **Cabin Security** – The last thing cabin crew members do right before takeoff is ensure that all seats are in an upright position, tray tables are appropriately folded up, hand baggage is properly stored, arm rests are down, and passenger seatbelts are all properly fastened.

6. **Cabin Inspections** – During the flight, cabin crew members should be alert for strange situations and sounds in the aircraft.

7. **Emergency** – It's essential for cabin crew members to have adequate first aid skills. They're also trained to handle several different types of emergency situations.

As mentioned above, cabin crew members also have customer care responsibilities in addition to ensuring passenger safety.

These responsibilities may include:

1. **Flight Briefing** – Cabin crew members are briefed on passengers who may have special requirements and are tasked to assist these passengers in boarding the aircraft.

2. **Flight Tasks** – Cabin crew members need to ensure that the aircraft is clean and tidy before passengers start boarding.

They're also responsible for ensuring that all stocks and meals are on board, and that all details and information provided in chair pockets are current.

3. **Welcoming Passengers** – Cabin crew members are responsible for welcoming passengers on board and making sure they leave the aircraft safe and sound when it reaches its destination.

4. **Serving Refreshments** – During the flight, cabin crew members are tasked to serve food and drinks to passengers.

5. **Offering Items for Sale** – Items such as alcohol, tobacco, and cologne are typically offered on board at duty-free rates, and the responsibility for offering these items to passengers also falls to cabin crew members.

6. **Post-flight Tasks** – Sometimes cabin crew members are responsible for tidying up the aircraft as soon as all passengers have disembarked. They are also tasked to make sure there's no luggage left inside the aircraft.

Basic Requirements

Other than the responsibilities above, here is a list of some additional requirements airlines look for:

1. **Education** – Every airline differs considerably on what education requirements it asks of prospective applicants so it best to check the individual airlines requirements before applying. And if you don't have the required education, but possess considerable customer service experience, some airlines may be willing to overlook your shortcomings.

2. **Health** – Good health is essential for cabin crew members. In fact, a medical assessment is often typically part of the entire selection process. Height and weight restrictions are also typically in place, and some airlines require the use of contact lenses for those with less than perfect eyesight. Check the individual airlines requirements before applying.

3. **Swimming Ability** – As a cabin crew candidate, you'll have to demonstrate your ability to swim at least twenty-five metres.

   Some airlines even require you to show you can swim for a minimum of thirty metres. Again check the individual airlines requirements before applying.

4. **Passport** – Cabin crew candidates also need to show proof that they're eligible to work and live in their country of residence and that they hold a valid passport, which allows them to travel without constraints.

5. **Customer Service Experience** – Customers are always the top priority of airline operators, which is why they often have a preference for applicants with sufficient customer service experience.

Of course, before you even start on the application process, make sure you've chosen the right airline and that you've done thorough research on your chosen airline to increase your chances of successfully landing a job.

Each airline has a different schedule of assessment and interview, but most of them are willing to spend money just to seek out the best talents from the four corners of the world.

What you need to do is let them know of your existence and the fact that you have the qualifications and talents that they're looking for. When these airlines come to your country looking to hire, be sure to go to the assessment day and make your presence known.

The Importance of Your Résumé

In applying for work as a flight attendant, remember that your résumé is of great importance. For one thing, only about five percent of applicants are invited to an interview. The other 95% are immediately rejected based on what the employer sees or doesn't see on their résumé. You should therefore take the necessary time and effort to prepare a powerful résumé. Strive to make yourself stand out right at the outset.

Remember there are probably a huge number of people with aviation experience vying for the same post.

Your Résumé

The fact that today's career world moves at a very fast pace makes your résumé a very important document indeed. It serves, among other things, as your passport to better career opportunities. Perhaps the most important thing you should take note of as regards your résumé is that there are no hard and fast rules in creating it. As we are all individuals, so too our résumés are unique. Of course, you'll have to plan, create, and use your résumé properly in order to take full advantage of it. You'll need to think very carefully about your personal attributes, professional skills, and career goals.

Before you start creating your résumé, you'll have to take a few basic rules into consideration as regards its construction. As mentioned earlier, each individual's résumé is different, but there are some general rules and principles that serve as the foundation for a good résumé.

First of all, bear in mind that your résumé should serve as a brochure, rather than an autobiography. Its primary purpose is not to tell your life story, but to help you land a job by selling your experience and skills to the prospective employer.

What is a Résumé Anyway?

Perhaps we should first answer this question to know exactly what you should be creating and how you should create it. The term "résumé" is a French.. The purpose of a résumé is to provide prospective employers with sufficient information about your skills and experience such that you catch their interest. There are different types of résumé and you'll have to choose the most appropriate type for your purposes. The aim should be for your résumé to bring you to the next step in the recruitment process, which is usually a formal interview.

Knowing What You Want

The first thing you need to do before actually creating your résumé is to set your career objectives. Remember that the more focused your objectives are, the higher your likelihood for success will be. You'll have to identify the things you find most fulfilling in your career and then analyse where you are right now in terms of achieving your career goals and where you want to go in the near future.

Here's how to properly set your career objectives:

1. Look at Your Career

Every individual has his own set of expectations regarding his career. For some people, success means moving upward to senior positions. For others, success means getting work that fits a particular lifestyle. Regardless of your priorities, you'll surely have some career highs as well as career lows. Analyzing where you are right now necessarily involves identifying these highs and lows.

2. Identify Your Objectives

Of course, you're the only one who can decide which of your objectives are absolutely essential and which are simply desirable.

What's important is that you're clear about what you believe is essential and that you understand that lifestyle considerations normally change from time to time. Your objectives will also become so much clearer to you and you'll be a lot more focused if you write them down on paper.

Creating Your Résumé

Remember that the primary role of your résumé is to make a prospective airline employer see your value, which means you really need to promote yourself. Creating a document that's nothing more than a career summary definitely won't sell your attributes and skills. This is why you need to think of your résumé more as a brochure than a biography. Creating a well-planned and error-free résumé also says a lot about your focus and motivation, which a prospective employer will surely appreciate.

Common Résumé Pitfalls

There are some general things you should and shouldn't do where your résumé is concerned. For one thing, it's a good idea to take a look at your friends' and colleagues' résumés if they're willing to show it to you. This'll give you an idea of what to include and what not to include in your own résumé.

You should also be honest about certain aspects of work that you normally don't enjoy or aren't very good at just yet.

Being straightforward is a trait many employers appreciate, as it shows that you're very objective about your capabilities. It's also a good idea to talk to others about your career goals so you can make sure you're moving towards the right direction.

What you should avoid when preparing your résumé is setting unrealistic goals, which will only lead you to disappointment. You should also avoid belittling your achievements and expertise.

Remember that you're trying to sell yourself to a prospective employer. If anyone needs to be confident about your skills and capabilities, then it should be you. After all, how can you convince an employer to hire you when you're not even sure of your own worth? More importantly, you shouldn't set negative objectives for yourself. A résumé is a document meant to help you move forwards, not backwards.

Looking Beyond the Obvious

If you want your résumé to be as effective as it can possibly be, then you need to gain a deeper understanding of how your prospective employers or recruiters are going to use it.

Always remember that an airline will look way beyond your qualifications and skills to determine if you're a good fit with the culture of their organization.

Remember as well that managers are likely to look for reasons to drop you from the list of qualified candidates, so make sure your application is error-free. Furthermore, bear in mind that your application documents will likely be read by different individuals with a different set of perspectives and attitudes. Even before you hand out your résumé, you should already have researched the company and ensured that you fit in with their culture.

Here are some tips to ensure application success:

1. Avoiding Red Flags

Unless you were born with a special lucky charm or possess some amazing and highly in-demand skills, then your résumé is likely to land on a reader's desk among many others.

Generally, an employer or recruiter decides whether to look for positive indicators in the résumé and select candidates in or identify red flags that can get an applicant rejected or selected out.

n many cases, the reader can choose to do both. Take note that many applications get rejected for the most trivial reasons, which is why you need to plan your résumé carefully and make sure it connects positively with your intended reader.

2. Scanner-Friendly

You may or may not realize this, but there are many large recruitment companies and airlines that scan résumé s into a recruitment system and personally check out only those that are short-listed by the computer.

What these recruitment systems do is identify keywords and phrases in a résumé and then matches them with the job requirements. It's therefore important for your résumé to be scanner-friendly.

Do this by making a list of the keywords and phrases covering your experience and skills, and then inserting them into your résumé. You should also make sure your résumé has a clear layout and that no unusual typefaces are used, as these may not be recognized by the scanner.

3. A Good Match

The primary basis for all good employment relationships is a good match between you, your job, and your organization's culture. This is what motivates you to become a committed employee and this is exactly what recruiters and prospective employers look for when they check your résumé.

The person screening your résumé will go beyond your skills and capability to do the job. He'll also try to gauge if you're the type of person who'll be compatible with the organization.

Therefore, you should make sure your résumé reaches out to the recruiter or prospective employer and speaks the language of the organization.

Identify Your Overlooked Skills

Your personal assets are made up of more than just your experience and qualifications. In fact, your behaviour is often a lot more important to airlines than your knowledge and skills.

Furthermore, prospective employers are likely to be more interested in what you can do for them in the future rather than what you've done for others in the past.

You'll therefore need to identify your transferable skills when preparing your résumé and this can be done by simply asking yourself the following questions:

1. Which of my skills lie behind the kind of work I enjoying doing the most?

2. Are there skills I use in my personal life that could be useful at work?

3. Whom can I ask for objective opinion about my transferable skills?

4. Which of my existing skills do I want to develop and re-use?

These overlooked qualities are often called transferable skills. So what are they exactly? Generally speaking, they are the underlying aspects of an individual that indicate how suited he is to a specific role. These skills have a lot to do with your personality, behaviour, motives, and values in addition to your experience and skills. In identifying your transferable skills, remember there will be those that aren't that easy to identify and hidden deep inside, but for purposes of your résumé, it's important that you do identify these skills.

Following are the four general categories of transferable skills:

Personal Qualities

- ➤ Interpersonal Sensitivity
- ➤ Flexibility
- ➤ Resilience
- ➤ Personal Motivation

Professional Qualities

- ➤ Specialist Knowledge
- ➤ Analysis and Problem Solving
- ➤ Oral and Written Communication

Managerial Qualities

- ➤ Leadership
- ➤ Planning and Organising
- ➤ Quality Orientation
- ➤ Persuasiveness

Entrepreneurial Qualities

- ➤ Commercial Awareness
- ➤ Innovation and Creativity
- ➤ Action Orientation
- ➤ Strategic Thinking

Your résumé largely depends on your assessment of yourself and your skills, which makes it a very subjective document. But, you should bear in mind that the more objective your résumé is, the more powerful it can be as well.

Therefore, you shouldn't just claim expertise on the transferable skills listed above, as practically anybody can do that.
Instead, you should demonstrate such expertise by pointing out past achievements that demonstrate those skills by giving examples.

Backing up your claims with a solid evidence of results makes you a whole lot more credible.

Here's a few ways to help you identify your transferable skills:

1. Listing Your Achievements

Identify at least 5 achievements you're particularly proud of, regardless of whether they have to do with your personal or professional life. Be very creative about what you count as an achievement and remember that they can go beyond the obvious. You may have responsibilities in your personal life that make use of skills you don't normally use at work. You may also have dealt with situations at one time or another that brought out talents and capabilities you weren't even aware you possessed.

2. Recognizing Overlooked Skills

To identify specific skills, the next thing you need to do is break your achievements down to component parts.

For each component part, think about what skills you needed to use. You should then specify the frequency with which you used each skill.

You may be surprised to find out that your personal life requires you to display a lot more skills than you use at work.

3. Rating Yourself

Using a scale of 1-5, where 1 is the lowest, rate how much you enjoyed using each of the identified skills and rate as well the degree to which you're looking forward to using the skill again.

Remember that there are times when you don't have to be very proficient at something in order to enjoy it. The next step won't be as easy, since it's basically a reality check. Therefore, it may be best to ask for the assistance of someone who knows you well so you can come up with a realistic rating for each skill.

4. Assessing the Results

Obviously, you should prioritize those skills you enjoy most and want to use again in your new job.

However, if you can only demonstrate limited evidence of these skills, then you may want to consider them as areas for career development.

Time to Create Your Résumé

Once you understand the basics of preparing your résumé, it's time to get down to the business of actually creating it. Set aside a considerable amount of time for writing, editing, and layout design in order to achieve maximum results.

Remember that your application documents are usually the first contact you ever have with a prospective employer. Consider as well that on first reading, these documents are likely to receive no more than 30 seconds of the prospective employer's time.

This is why you need to make sure your résumé has the right kind of information written in the right order and presented in a manner that's easy to read and understand.

Your résumé should help you create a good first impression and every single part of your application documents should invite the reader to continue reading.

This means your cover letter should be succinct and relevant enough that the reader will be convinced to check out your résumé.

The front page of your résumé should then be written such that the reader will be encouraged to look beyond your qualifications and your current position. Remember that your goal is for the first impression to get your application placed on the "interested" pile.

Make sure your résumé lets the reader know immediately why you're the right choice for the flight attendant job you're applying for and for their organization in general.

When deciding on which particular pieces of information to include in your résumé first and the order in which you should write them, always remember that the résumé is intended for the reader, not for you.

Therefore, you should do your best to judge the importance of each piece of information through your target reader's eyes.

For example, you may have impressive educational achievements, but if you're aware that a prospective employer doesn't really care much about this, then it's best to delegate that piece of information to the latter pages of your résumé.

Another thing that may seem trivial, but can actually affect the results of your résumé considerably is its length. The general rule is to prepare a two-page résumé, but a three-page résumé is also acceptable in exceptional circumstances. This means that in two short pages, you should be able to provide a convincing summary of your achievements, experience, and qualifications.

You should also be able to provide sufficient personal details to convince the reader that you're worth seeing in the next step of the recruitment process.

A third page in your résumé is generally deemed acceptable when you're required to list down technical skills or publications. Make sure you rigorously edit out anything that may be deemed irrelevant.

Quick Tips for Writing Your Résumé

1. Use paper of good quality and a clear and pleasing layout to show that you're organized and business-like.

2. Write in a style that's easy to read to show that you have good writing and communication skills.

3. Provide information on complicated matters in a clear and simple manner to show you're a concise thinker.

4. Edit your résumé and make sure there aren't any grammatical or spelling mistakes to show you pay close attention to detail.

5. Cite appropriate employment history and qualifications to prove that you're qualified for the job.

Describing Yourself

You generally use only about a hundred words to describe yourself in your résumé.

Take note, though, that these words leave a critical impression on your readers, who typically draw conclusions that are just as critical.

Therefore, just like every other aspect of your résumé, you need to plan this portion of the document with as much precision as possible. In describing yourself, remember it isn't just what you say that's important, it's also how you say it.

A lot of job applicants stick to old-fashioned and overly formal writing styles in creating their résumé and cover letters. Some people even write their résumé in the third person. What you should do, instead, is write your résumé in a plain and jargon-free language that puts more emphasis on the content, rather than the style.

Being Yourself

Your name is, of course, the very first thing you write on your résumé.

If you have professional accreditations and qualifications, then you'll have to consider whether indicating them after your name is a good idea or not.

As a general rule, you should include only those qualifications and accreditations that are relevant to the work you're applying for.

Giving Contact Details

Another thing you should ensure when preparing your résumé is to make it as easy as possible for the reader to contact you. Obviously, it's necessary to provide your full address.

If you spend most of the day away from home, then you should indicate this fact and provide an alternative means to contact you. It's best to provide as many telephone contact points as possible; provide a work number if it's okay to take calls there and a mobile number if you have one. If you have regular access to email, then it's best to indicate your email address as well.

Your Age

In the United States, it's not necessary for you to indicate your age in your résumé. But this piece of information is actually considered relevant in other countries.

So check what is appropriate for your country. Besides, the reader can take an educated guess at your age from other pieces of information and dates indicated in your résumé.

The general rule you should follow is to indicate your age on the first page of your résumé if you believe it is significant to your application. Otherwise, it's best to list it under "Other Personal Information."

Cultural Differences

Remember that each country has its own conventions and general rules as regards the preparation of a résumé. In the US, for example, there are very strict laws governing the pieces of information an employer is entitled to know about you. In Europe, it's common practice to include a photograph, particularly in the Benelux countries and in Germany. It's also customary to include detailed descriptions of your schooling and higher education. In Japan and in the Far East, there are instances when only graduates of certain universities are allowed to apply to particular employers.

These cultural differences, along with other considerations, may be important when you're providing details of your home life in your résumé. Among the other considerations you may find difficult to decide on is your civil status.

For example, as you're applying for a flight attendants job, being single may seem like a huge advantage as you don't have to worry so much about leaving a spouse for long periods of time. On the other hand, if the job requires someone secured and settled, then married individuals may seem ideal.

The truth, however, is that neither assumption is necessarily correct. If you do decide to include your civil status in your résumé, then you need to ask yourself what conclusions a reader might draw from it.

You should also reflect on whether this piece of information is indeed relevant to your application. Finally, it's best to indicate your marital status on the last page of your résumé regardless of how relevant you may think it is.

To successfully apply the above guidelines, it may be a good idea to ask yourself these questions after completing the first draft of your résumé:

1. Does my résumé sound like me and can I proudly say that it reflects who I am?

2. Do I really want to be contacted at work or can that possibly jeopardize my position?

3. Is everything on my résumé easily understood?

4. Are there any other pieces of personal information that are particularly relevant to my application?

5. Do the interests and pieces of personal information I provided give an impression I can easily justify and am happy with?

Your Interests

The things you do in your spare time say a great deal about you. You should therefore bear in mind that the interests you list down in your résumé help paint a picture of the kind of person you are for the reader.

Interests like rock climbing suggest that you're an active individual, while such pursuits as archaeology indicate an enquiring mind. Fondness for DIY projects may indicate the virtue of being practical, while interest in music indicates creativity.

Whatever interests you decide to include, make sure they're relevant and that they emphasize the useful skills you've mastered that may also be relevant to the job you're applying for.

Portray a Positive Image

Always remember that recruitment is basically all about discrimination – particularly discrimination in favour of the most suitable candidate.

This is why your résumé has to be written such that the reader will be convinced you are the best candidate for the job.

Take note, however, that there will always be some readers who succumb to less constructive bias and these readers will make presumptions from the personal information you include in your résumé.

In fact, it may be possible for the reader to draw the wrong conclusions about your gender, your race, and your sexual orientation from what you in include or leave out of your résumé.

You should therefore be careful not to give out information that can possibly be negatively misconstrued.

In summary, here are some important points to remember when preparing your résumé:

- ➢ Listing down too many time-consuming interests may give the reader the impression that you have little time for work.
- ➢ The reader may interpret your interests negatively.

- ➤ Prospective employers are only interested in your home life in as far as its impact on your work.
- ➤ Prospective employers are likely to draw conclusions regarding the kind of person you are based on your interests.
- ➤ It's important to highlight any achievements or personal successes outside your workplace.

Other than the points listed above, it's also important to make it clear to the reader why he should take your application seriously. As much as possible, you should avoid putting yourself in a situation where you can be rejected simply because of a misunderstanding as regards your circumstances.

Education and Training

Your achievements, whether gained through education or training, represent both your acquired knowledge and your ability to develop as an individual. Understand that many employers spend a considerable amount of money on employee training, which is why they want to make sure you're worth the investment.

Detailing Your Education

There's a very simple guideline for describing your education in your résumé: The more recent your education is, the more complete your description should be. Think about it this way: When you're 29, your education naturally forms an important part of your personal achievements.

As such, it'll be of significant interest to a prospective employer. But, when you're 43, your work history will be of far more importance than your education, which will mostly be of passing interest to prospective employers.

As far as both your educational and professional qualifications are concerned, the guideline is quite similar: The more recent and relevant a qualification is, the more complete your description should be and the earlier it should appear on you résumé. You should then leave less recent and less relevant qualifications to the last page. Remember that this part is your first opportunity to highlight your personal achievements.

Showing Career Development

If you have formal professional qualifications, then you need to include the details of these qualifications with your education history.

However, details of other training don't necessarily have to appear on the first page of your résumé unless they're critical to your job application.

It may be wise to consider including a "Professional and Personal Development" section on the second page, where you may include details of formal training and other initiatives for which you may not have a certificate, but which may be important for career development.

And if your training record is impressive, then you may mention the topics and dates, but only of the most recent and relevant ones, of course.

To make sure you present your achievements and qualifications in the best light, it's best to bear in mind the following dos and don'ts:

- ✓ Consider how relevant your academic record is to your prospective employer.

- ✓ Include all special citations in courses or examinations that are relevant to the job you're applying for.
- ✓ Use positive language in this section of your résumé.

- ✗ Don't indicate subjects you've taken, but are weak in.

- ✗ Exclude training that has no bearing whatsoever on your application.

- ✗ Avoid going into unnecessary detail.

Among the most important things to remember when you're preparing your résumé is that your experience and skills shouldn't be lost in a sea of irrelevant information.

Always remember that space is very precious in a résumé and unless a prospective employer specifically requests it or it's particularly relevant to the position you're applying for, then details on your health, your religion, passport number, political affiliation, driver's license details, nationality, place of birth and next of kin should be excluded.

Make Your Experience Stand Out

Your résumé necessarily includes not just a description of yourself and your qualifications, but also a section meant to convince a prospective employer that you have the best experience and attitude for the job.

Towards that purpose, you'll need to use a jargon-free, positive, and concise language in this part of your résumé. In order to sell your experience successfully, you'll have to carefully consider not only the facts that you include, but also the vocabulary and tone you use.

Remember as well that your résumé will reflect your career in retrospect for the most part, so it's advisable to use the past tense. It's best, however, to use the present tense when describing current challenges. Be careful not to use I, me, or my too much, as these can make you sound boastful and over-confident.

You should strive to prepare your résumé such that it becomes an objective appraisal of your abilities. Focus on the type of words you should use when describing your experience in your résumé.

Compiling a list of suitable words may be a good idea. Remember that you need to exude just the right amount of confidence in both your résumé and cover letter, and the best way to do this is to use positive language.

Check each sentence in your résumé carefully and remove any unnecessary or irrelevant word or phrase. Also it's a good idea to make a list of alternative words and phrases so as to avoid repetition.

Tell Them About Your Experience

An important part of selling your experience to prospective employers is an effective description. Take note that a straightforward enumeration of the things you did and whom you did them for may not be enough. You must present a record of your achievements to the reader such that he'll appreciate what you can do for his or her own organization in the future. You should also remember that an event won't have any significance to an employer without an outcome. It's also important to add some quantifying details between the event itself and the outcome so the employer can see what's in it for him.

Describing Achievements and Responsibilities

Among the most common complaints of employers about résumé is that they're usually nothing more than a series of job descriptions. Bear in mind a prospective employer needs to know what you did and how well you did it. Job descriptions may be useful, but they serve a different purpose in your résumé and prospective employers are often more interested in your abilities because they point to the future rather than the past.

In order to land the new job you're eyeing, you'll need to place careful thought to what your résumé says about your responsibilities and achievements in your current and past jobs.

Take note as well that the culture of your present organization may be of particular interest to a prospective employer, but you should use specialist terms only if you're sure the résumé reader will understand them.

How to Speak About Success

As previously mentioned, any success you describe in your résumé should be quantified and properly supported by outcomes in order for a prospective employer to understand how it could benefit them.

For example, the statement:

"Sold new product to supplier"

could be improved to:

"I sold 5 blue widgets for a 6-month subscription worth $100,000. The product users' experienced 40% efficiency gains from the new product."

The improved ultra-specific statement assures the reader that the stated success isn't something you just made up.

Employer Information

Never assume that a prospective employer is familiar with your past and present employers.

Even if you've worked for a well-known organization, it isn't likely that your new prospect will know much about the department you work or worked in.

Therefore, it's essential to provide a brief description of the company's core activity and throw in some important details as well. These details may include sales turnover, profits, number of employees, and any other piece of information that's relevant.

This is also a good place in your résumé to hint at the corporate health of the organization at the time you worked there. This can effectively put your experience into the context for the reader. Remember as well that two individuals with the same job description may have completely different experiences and employers want to know in what kind of environment you're used to working.

How to Use Job Titles

While it's important to write down job details clearly, it's equally important to list job titles just as clearly.

Each organization may have a different meaning for a job title, so it's best to use generic job titles wherever possible.

You'll also need to provide a summary of your responsibilities and one way of doing this is by giving a one or two sentence description under a heading like "Responsibilities" or "Accountabilities." Finally, try not to state the obvious too much while still making sure that all interesting, unusual, and unique aspects of your work are included.

Delivering Dates

Résumé readers normally don't like gaps, so what should you do if your career has them?

First of all, you need to remember that while it's important to demonstrate a clear record of career progression, you really don't have to account for every single month of your career. It's therefore wise to stick to years when you provide your employment dates in your résumé. If you had more than one job or position with the same employer, then it's best to use an overall heading for the employer, stating your joining and leaving dates.

You may then enter each role as a sub-heading and provide dates for each as well. Be careful not to hint at being currently unemployed even if you are.

In preparing this part of your résumé, ask yourself if you've covered all periods of employment and if you've perhaps included too many irrelevant details about any of your jobs.

You also need to reflect on whether you've been consistent in your use of headings and bulleted points, and if the language of your résumé is positive without being overbearing.

The importance of your bulleted points lies in the fact that they're basically an invitation for the reader to focus on that particular part of your résumé and helps him scan your work experience.

Remember to start each bullet point with a positive action word and group your achievements under numbered paragraphs wherever appropriate.

Same Employer. Different Job?

There may have been certain points in your life when you worked several different jobs in quick succession.

If these jobs were with the same employer, then it's wise to group them together under one heading and emphasize the range of experience you've gained from them. However, you must make it clear to your reader that you weren't simply moved around due to attitude problems and that the high number of roles doesn't necessarily indicate your inability to settle in any post.

If the successive jobs were with different employers, then you'll have to indicate if they were of a permanent nature or a series of temporary jobs. Try your best not to deliver a negative message because of too much movement in your career.

Past Work

As you progress through your résumé, your descriptions of previous employment should gradually become shorter.

Only your most recent jobs are in need of full descriptions of your responsibilities and achievements. While a particular achievement in a job you had ten years ago may be something you're extremely proud of, it may not really be of much interest to your résumé reader.

In fact, you really shouldn't bother describing previous employment that's irrelevant to your current application; giving the dates of employment and name of your employer should suffice. Remember that selecting the right kind of information to include in your résumé demonstrates good judgement to a potential employer.

Temporary Positions

Many people get into temporary employment for whatever reason at some point in their careers. You may have done the same thing to fund higher education or simply to gain work experience. Temporary jobs may even have served as stop-gaps between permanent jobs. In preparing your résumé, you shouldn't feel obliged to describe each of these jobs in detail.

Prospective employers are likely more interested in the commitment and initiative you demonstrate by taking on temporary work.

You may also treat this as an opportunity to showcase a diverse range of experiences, which you've gained from various work assignments and environments.

Choosing a Look for Your Résumé

Although there isn't really a right way to structure your résumé, there are several things you need to avoid.

Remember that visual layout could be the most subjective aspect of your résumé, but the objective should always be to ensure that it's user-friendly and can be scanned easily by the reader's eyes. In general, a simple layout that does away with too many heading levels or type styles is the most effective.

In preparing your résumé layout, you should remember that you're not aiming for a design award, but for legibility and clarity. More importantly, you should never underestimate the power of a pleasing and well-presented résumé.

Layout and structure

There are generally three core elements you need to consider when structuring your résumé and each element has to be distinctly recognizable to the reader. The first element is the contact and other personal information that are important enough to indicate on the first page. The second element is your relevant employment history and the third element is any other relevant personal information.

Typeface

Where choosing a typeface is concerned, it's best to keep things simple and to remember that using fancy typefaces won't do your application any good.

Furthermore, if you email your résumé, you can't be sure the recipient's computer is set-up for fancy typefaces. And if your résumé is subjected to electronic scanning, then you'll have a greater chance of getting selected in with a simple typeface. And remember you should use only one typeface for the entire résumé.

Type size

This is another important consideration when preparing your résumé. Choosing a point size that's too large will only waste valuable space, whereas choosing a point size too small can make your text appear dense and quite difficult for the reader to decipher.

Paper

It's likely that your résumé will be handled by several individuals, so the quality of paper and envelopes you use is really very important. Paper that's too thin will look tatty, while paper that's too thick is likely to be permanently creased by the time the intended reader receives it.

It's generally advisable to use A4-sized (or the US letter equivalent) paper of good quality that's coloured white. It's also a good idea to choose photocopier-friendly paper. And if you have to send your résumé via post, be sure to fold it only once and enclose it in an appropriately-sized envelope.

Templates

Many of the available word processing packages include templates for résumés, which can make layout so much easier for you, so you may want to consider using them. However, you should be careful not to use a system that wastes too much space or prompts you to include unnecessary information.

Remember as well that standard templates are just that – standard. Your résumé needs to be unique and interesting, so always remember that the template should help only with the layout and not with the content.

Résumé Quality Control

Preparing the content and layout of your résumé takes up so much time, which is why you need to get it right.

After writing the first draft of your résumé, it's important to check the document thoroughly for any mistake and it may even be a good idea to let a friend give it the once-over.

Here are some important points to remember when conducting quality control for your résumé:

- ➤ All information specifically requested by a prospective employer should be included.

- ➤ Employers won't be satisfied with knowing what you've done; they'll also want to know how well you did it.

- ➤ If a prospective employer requires salary details, don't forget to include important perks and bonuses.

- ➤ Be sure to act on useful feedback from friends, colleagues, employers, and recruiters.

- ➤ The key interest points in your résumé for prospective employers are your achievements and transferable skills.

And now for a list of things you need to avoid when preparing your résumé:

✗ Do not lie

Naturally, your résumé is going to be a positive statement about your career. But, bear in mind that there's a clear line between positive presentation and misrepresentation, and you should take care never to step across that line. Don't claim any qualifications you don't have, indicate courses you haven't really attended, or include work you never did. If an employer ever finds out you did any of these things, they're entitled to cancel your employment contract and you may even get blacklisted as a result.

✗ Do not mention salary details

The résumé reader is typically concerned only about assessing your suitability for a job, so remuneration isn't really that relevant. Of course, there may be instances when a prospective employer specifically asks for salary details or a record of your salary progression. In that case, you should provide the necessary information in your cover letter rather than the résumé itself.

✗ Do not include a photograph

As long as you've ensured that your résumé's content is well-planned, well-prepared, and well-thought out, then you should be assured that it'll give the reader a positive and objective opinion of you. Attaching a photograph to your résumé may just succeed in tempting a reader to make subjective decisions based on nothing more than your appearance. Of course, if you're applying for work in the fashion industry, then a photograph may be a requirement.

Asking for a Outside Help

It's not easy to choose someone to read your résumé and give you an honest opinion on whether it's good or not. It's only logical to look for someone who's familiar with the kind of work you do and understands the underlying concepts of the field you're in.

People are often a little meek when writing about themselves, so you'll likely be encouraged by your résumé editor to be more outgoing and to highlight your good points to the fullest.

Keep an open mind and listen very carefully to all the feedback you get, and then decide what changes you need to make in order to improve your résumé.

Aside from getting feedback, here are some important dos and don'ts to remember when finalizing your résumé:

- ✓ Check the spelling, punctuation, and use of tenses in your résumé.

- ✓ Make sure you use action words and positive phrases in both your résumé and cover letter.

- ✓ Adjust your résumé to fit every situation or job you're applying for.

- ✗ Try not to undersell yourself.

- ✗ Never forget how important first impressions are.

- ✗ Don't include references unless a prospective employer specifically asks for them; they're usually requested at a later date.

Adapting Your Résumé

To truly make your résumé effective, you need to think of it as an evolving document and understand that the different résumé styles are appropriate for different instances.

Your résumé should keep evolving, in the same way that your life keeps moving. And just as different individuals see different sides of your personality at different occasions, your résumé should also change according to the circumstances.

What Type of Résumé to Write

Most people write their résumé and then simply modify the same document as they experience changes in their careers. What you need to do, instead, is prepare a different résumé at different times in your life.

There are times when you may need to sell your employment history in order to land a new job. At another time, the requirement may be for you to sell your skills and potential.

Remember, though, that your transferable skills are almost always the factor that wins you the job. Remember as well that it's important to support whatever skills you wish to sell in your résumé with concrete evidence of their use.

When choosing the right résumé for a particular application, ask yourself these questions:

1. Am I seeking a change of direction in my career?

2. Have I prepared a list of career objectives and transferable skills, which I can readily refer to?

3. Do my experiences and skills match the job I'm currently applying for?

What Approach to Take

The approach you take in putting your résumé together should be dictated in large part by the job you're applying for, the person who's going to read the résumé, and the kind of person they're looking for.

Always remember that no two jobs are ever the same and you don't just leave one job to perform the exact same functions in another company. Therefore, it's only logical that one résumé won't be right for all job applications. Whether you make slight modifications to your résumé or prepare an entirely new one, you'll have to change your approach each time so as to meet the demands of each application. Skilfully tailoring your résumé to fit a particular application also helps you highlight the specific skills and range of experience that a prospective employer is looking for.

To make sure your résumé is appropriately tailored to the application, list down the relevant skills and experience required for the job, review your career objectives, and then adapt them accordingly. As always, it's a good idea to get a second opinion on what impression your résumé inspires in a reader.

4 Ways to Find a Job

So, you already have your résumé prepared and you've made sure it's as error-free as it can ever be.

But, how exactly do you make your résumé work to your advantage?

Before you go out on a job-hunting trip, make sure you're familiar with every single method you can use to secure your dream job.

There are generally four methods for securing a job and it's important that you make good use of every single one of them.

1. Replying to Advertisements

There are thousands of job advertisements being placed in different media throughout the year. Newspapers, magazines, journals, and the Internet abound with job advertisements you can check. This is in fact the most accessible market for jobs you can find.

Take note, though, that this is also the most competitive market, so you'll have to really sell yourself well if you choose to go this route. The good thing is that you're sure the advertisers are really committed to recruiting the best applicant for the advertised post.

2. Recruitment

Generally, the logic behind recruitment companies is that they find people for jobs, rather than jobs for people. They are paid to shortlist qualified candidates for certain positions, who will then go through the final selection process.

There are companies that operate databases and there are also those that headhunt or advertise for specific posts. It's advantageous for you to make use of both types of recruitment companies.

3. On spec

If you already have a clear idea of what specific work you want to do and which particular company or individual you want to do it for, then this may be the best route for you.

The key to success with this method is in approaching the right person with a clear proposition. And even if your target company already holds you in their database, you should still continue monitoring their job advertisements.

4. Network to get work

Someone you know just might know someone looking to recruit a person with your qualifications. So, you shouldn't hesitate to talk to your circle of friends and associates when you're looking for a new job.

Of course, you'll have to do this pro-active job hunt in a discreet manner. This method can be time-consuming, but it can also be very effective, especially for those who are just starting out in their careers or returning to work after a hiatus.

Getting Your Résumé Out There

You've spent so much time and effort on your résumé that it's imperative that it does its job of earning you interviews.

To successfully achieve that purpose, you need to send it to the right people and with the right cover letter.

As you probably know, job advertisements represent what's probably the most open recruitment marketplace.

As such, it's a highly competitive field and your application will really need to work hard for you when you reply to any job advertisement. Remember that the careful preparation of a cover letter is just as important as your résumé when you reply to advertisements.

Match Making

Remember that job advertisements typically provide very limited information about the employer and the specific role of the person they're looking for.

The challenge for you, then, is to mark advertisements that look interesting, look beyond the words used on the advertisement, analyse the employer's needs, and see if your qualifications and skills match the criteria you come up with.

The more precisely your skills match up with a job, the greater your chances are of getting shortlisted. The general rule of thumb is for your qualifications and skills to exceed 80% of the advertised requirements.

Following Instructions

When replying to a job advertisement, be sure to read the reply instructions very carefully. You may not know this, but among the most common reasons for job applicants getting rejected at first selection is that they didn't follow reply instructions.

Employers and recruitment agencies will likely ask you to quote a reference number and they may also ask for other pieces of information, such as your expectations of the job and your salary progressions.

It's very rare that an employer will contact you to ask for information you've omitted, since they're likely to have plenty of other applicants who have followed the reply instructions to the letter.

Getting Past the First Selection

One thing that is vital to understand is that your résumé isn't likely to get more than a 30-second glance the very first time a reader lays eyes on it.

You'll have to make sure your résumé passes this at-a-glance test and makes it to the next round by ensuring that you've done the following:

- ✓ Strictly followed reply instructions
- ✓ Ensured that overall presentation is good
- ✓ Used a clear writing style
- ✓ Shown good attention to detail
- ✓ Displayed good judgement by choosing the right relevant information
- ✓ Presented information succinctly

Remember as well that employers and recruitment companies receive hundreds of applications each day, so you'll have to find ways of making your application stand out.

One effective way of doing this is to make sure your application is easily searchable by scanning software, which is often used by large companies to make the process of sifting through hundreds of applications easier.

How do you make your résumé searchable?

If the job posting indicates that the main requirements for the available position are team-building experience and leadership skills, then you'd do well to edit your résumé to highlight these skills.

It won't hurt to use the specific terms used in the job posting wherever appropriate.

We Are All Different

You should also bear cultural differences in mind when preparing your application documents. For instance, there are countries where a written cover letter is expected rather than a typewritten one. The best example of this is perhaps France, where written cover letters are preferred by employers because these are usually sent to a hand writing expert, whose job is to draw up a characterisation of the applicant by analysing the application.

Staying Organized

It's also important for you to keep track of your applications so you'll always be prepared for your next move.

Here are some dos and don'ts for the effective use of your résumé:

- ✓ Keep dated copies of all job advertisements you reply to.

- ✓ Check if there's a closing date on the advertisement and be sure to reply with plenty of time.

- ✓ Write a relevant cover letter for each application.

- ✓ Make sure your application passes the 30-second test.

- ✗ The world shouldn't stop if you get rejected. Just accept the fact and then move on to the next application.

- ✗ Don't just apply for jobs indiscriminately. Instead, you have to make sure each application you make is focused.

- ✗ Don't ignore reply instructions.

- ✗ Don't omit information that was specifically requested.

Writing Your Cover Letter

Job advertisements are very carefully worded so as to attract the most suitable applicants. Therefore, when you reply to an advertisement, your cover letter needs to show the reader that you understand perfectly the nature of the advertised job.

The letter should also summarize why your application deserves to be given serious consideration. Pick out the experience and key skills required for the position and then allow your letter to demonstrate how you match those requirements.

Similar to when you're preparing your résumé, you need to pay close attention to details and provide strong evidence of your suitability for the job.

Specifically, here's what you need to do in your cover letter:

> ➢ Quote the job title and reference numbers at the start of your cover letter.

- ➢ Use the first name if it's indicated in the advertisement.

- ➢ Highlight your understanding of the prospective employers business.

- ➢ Illustrate relevant achievements, particularly those that demonstrate the key skills for the job.

- ➢ Highlight any experience you've had of leading a successful team.

- ➢ Show motivation and an inherent belief in career possibilities.

- ➢ Demonstrate commitment and empathy.

Creating a Speculative Letter

When you write your speculative letter, try to put yourself in the recipients' shoes and bear in mind that they typically receive hundreds or even thousands of such letters each day.

As much as possible, open your letter with a positive statement. You may then move on to describe the key aspects of your résumé in a succinct manner and emphasize why the person should take interest in you.

Finally, your proposition must be clear and you should leave the reader in no doubt about what your career objectives are. Make sure your speculative letter is straightforward and that it clearly states your strengths as well as the type of jobs you want to be considered for.

Getting Feedback

In case your application is rejected at the first stage, the best course of action is simply to accept that there were better qualified candidates than yourself. There are times, however, when you just feel that you fit the job specifications so closely that it's just so difficult to understand what went wrong. While you shouldn't question the recruiter's judgement, it's quite okay to ask for an explanation. You may request constructive feedback about their reason for rejecting your application and how you may present your case better in the future.

Following Up

If you've given a speculative letter to a company, then it's only logical to expect a response from them. As much as possible, of course, you'd want the response to be an invitation to an exploratory meeting, but sometimes the response can simply be an undertaking to hold your details on file.

If you've heard nothing from the company after three months or so, then you should consider contacting them again and sending an updated résumé.

And because your flight attendant job search will likely stretch over several months, it's a good idea to keep a record of your contacts as well as any follow-up communication you've sent so the whole process becomes less stressful.

Using the Internet to Boost Your Chances of Job Success

It can't be denied that the Internet is currently the fastest-growing medium of recruitment and email is increasingly being used in most areas of recruitment.

The Internet allows you to access jobs from all over the world. But, because the Internet is such a huge resource, you need to use it selectively to achieve the best results. The Internet may indeed be rewriting the manner of conducting business in several fields, but the basic rules of recruitment are still the same.

You're still likely to come across your next job via job advertisements, personal networking, or simply sending in your application on paper. However the internet does change the way companies communicate, thus giving you more opportunities to network and greater access to more jobs.

When looking for flight attendant jobs on the Internet, there are generally two types of websites you can check.

1. A job site can either be specialist or non-specialist and some are nothing more than notice boards. Major job sites will typically have thousands of vacancies across several countries or continents.

It's a good idea to begin by limiting your flight attendant job search according to the type of vacancy or by location. The good thing is that many of these sites have search facilities that can help refine your search.

2. The second type of site is the corporate site, which is specific to one company and often used as a promotional tool. These sites not only advertise vacancies often, but are also great sources of background information on a company. They may even offer opportunities for you to leave your details.

Sneaky Trick

When people look for jobs online, many of them tend to look for just one job and then give up when they don't find it. What you need to do is look under more than just one job title. There may be companies looking for someone to fill the exact role you have in mind, but under a different job title, so ask yourself what else your chosen career may be called and then conduct an online search with those titles.

If you really want to wait for the perfect job to come along, then you may want to set up "Google Alerts" to send you daily emails with updates on your flight attendant job search terms. Search "Google Alerts" and follow the simple online instructions.

Researching Airlines Online

Just as the Internet provides access to a wide range of jobs, it also allows you to research not only a company's career opportunities, but also its products, services, and locations.

This is important for sorting out the employers who specifically need your qualifications and skills as well as for identifying which employers you'd most enjoy working for. Among other things, you should study the background of their key management officials, the statements made by management, and their economic history.

With this information, you'll be able to draft a more focused cover letter and face an interview with confidence.

How to Use Email to Get a Flight Attendant Job

Email can be very useful for finding jobs through the Internet, but you'll have to be careful in using it. There may have been a number of times when you received an unclear email where you couldn't really understand what the other person was trying to say.

There may also have been times when you automatically deleted an email without opening it simply because the sender's name sounded unfamiliar. So bear in mind that you'll need to make sure your own emailed application and cover letter doesn't get deleted for the same reasons.

Here are some tips on how you can ensure job success via email:

1. **Use a professional email address**

   This definitely isn't the time for you to use a silly or funny email address. It's best to use your full name as your email address for job hunting purposes.

This makes it easier for a company's hiring manager to recognize your email when he looks through his account. If your email is difficult to see at a glance, then the hiring manager may never find it.

2. **Check your P's and Q's**

This is the perfect time to show off your writing skills and fluency in the English language. Among other things, you'll want to assure the prospective employer that you did graduate successfully from school or college.

Take note that email applications reflect not only your intellect, but also your personality. Spelling, grammar, and punctuation errors can easily give the impression of laziness on your part.

3. **Check your sentence structure**

Be sure to use proper sentence structure whenever you type an email for application purposes.

Never use fragmented sentences or run-on sentences. You should also choose a font that's large and clear enough for the email recipient to read. It's also advised that you use only black text in your email. It bears reminding once again that this isn't the time to be different or silly.

4. **Check the signature block**

The signature block can be used effectively to highlight your expertise. Choose an appropriate salutation and then place your name and degree conferred after it.

It's also a good idea to provide your phone number below the signature block so the reader can easily contact you. If you have a blog or website that is relevant to your application, then it's also a good idea to list the URL in your signature block.

Email as Cover Letter

Treat your email as the cover letter for your résumé, since it's the first thing a prospective employer will see.

Therefore, you need to take as much care in writing the email as you would writing a cover letter to be sent through post. The tone of your email cover letter should also be one of a formal business letter, rather than the usual casual informality that's come to be associated with email in general.

Many email systems also allow you to request for a receipt to be sent once is delivered to the recipient or opened and read. It's indeed wise for you to do this, since job applications are important documents. And because it's an automatic function, the recipient doesn't have to be bothered in the process.

When sending an email, it's advisable to send your résumé as an attachment. Of course, you'll need to be familiar with what word-processing packages can easily be opened by the intended recipient. You should also take note of certain conventions regarding page layout. In the United States, for example, the standard setup is to use US letter rather than A4.

More importantly, you shouldn't send your résumé as a text-only document because that will make your application look just like all the others. As much as possible, you'd want your application to stand out from the rest.

Furthermore, you should ensure that all information included in your email is accurate and appropriate and that you won't mind having your name attached to it, regardless of who reads it.

Companies naturally want to make sure any individual they hire will project the right image for their business, which is why it's very important to be professional. And as mentioned earlier, your email address is also something you need to take into serious consideration. You may have to create a professional email to use solely for career purposes.

Here are some tips in creating a professional-sounding email address:

1. Avoid including anything that may reveal your age, such as your year of birth. Although it's illegal in many countries for employers to discriminate against applicants based on their age, it's a sad reality that such discrimination still exists.

2. Avoid any reference to gender, religion, or political affiliations, regardless of how passionate you are about it. After all, you're not aiming to be hired for what you believe in, but for what you can do.

3. You should also be careful about including health references in your email address. Although surviving an illness is indeed great news, it can raise concerns in a prospective employer as regards health costs and may in some cases cause your application to get rejected.

4. Keep it simple. A prospective employer definitely won't appreciate receiving email from someone whose email address looks like some alien code.

   Make your email address easy to remember. Your safest bet, of course, is your name. It makes the reader feel as if you're talking directly to him and vice versa.

Getting Social to Find a Flight Attendant Job

Using social networks can be a very effective job search tool. Social networking can be very effective primarily because it's so much easier to get positive results with several people helping you find the best career opportunities.

And in this day and age, social media may be the best way to get other people involved in your flight attendant job search.

The top three social media sites you can take advantage of for this purpose are LinkedIn, Facebook, and Twitter.

Here's how:

LinkedIn

This can be the best place to start where flight attendant job searches are concerned. The site allows you to see the profiles of other users and even connect with them. One very effective way of using LinkedIn is to keep an updated repository for the contact information of friends and colleagues who've moved on to other careers. When you're looking for a new job, you may then use this contact information to let your network know exactly what you're looking for. Many people get good leads through LinkedIn.

Take note that your profile is the first thing a prospective employer sees when they connect with you on LinkedIn, so it's best to create as professional one as you can. You'll know your profile is successful if you receive introductions, invitations to chat, or even invitations to an interview.

If you don't get the response you expect, then take a good look at your profile and consider revising it.

Treat your profile as a marketing tool that should entice readers to learn more about you.

Facebook

This is perhaps the most popular social networking site on earth at the moment. But did you know it could be used for job search too. The good thing about Facebook is that you can inform friends and colleagues about your flight attendant job search and let other people get to know you better as well. People who read your posts and receive your requests for help may not only provide you with good leads, but also give you valuable advice and encourage you as you continue with your flight attendant job search.

Twitter

This can be very effective for connecting with people sharing the same interests as yours. You have the option of following people involved in the kind of work you're interested in and talk about your flight attendant job search while you're at it. Other tweeters may even give you some valuable advice. A tool called Twello can also help you search through URLs and profiles to find company names you're interested in.

The tool also helps you find new people to follow and connect with.

An estimated 200 million people are now using Twitter and the employers and recruitment companies you're interested in are surely among them. You can keep up-to-date on these organisations by using the hash tag.

You also have the option of posting your résumé on your own Internet site or blog. This is ideal for you if you're free to conduct a public job search without risk of possible repercussions from your current employment. This option may require some specialist instructions, but it still represents ultimate self-promotion. As a job seeker, remember that you'll need to reach out to other people for help and you'll need to go about it in a professional yet creative manner.

Preparing for the Interview

If you're lucky enough to get to the interview part of the selection process, then you need to prepare for it by conducting a thorough research on the travel industry, particularly the airline you're applying for work in.

The interviewers will definitely expect you to know a lot about them, their routes, the number of people they employ, the cost of their flights, their customer base, and the services offered on their flights, among other things.

Whether you're going for an initial or a second interview, remember to leave home early. This helps you avoid being late for the interview in case you run into traffic problems or experience difficulties in finding parking space. Arriving early for interviews also gives you an edge because people are naturally impressed by punctuality.

It is often said that it takes only two seconds for a person to form a first impression of someone else and as you've probably heard before, first impressions usually last. Therefore, you definitely want to make a good first impression when you attend a job interview.

Remember too that first impressions are generally based on your appearance, the clothes you wear, your manner of speaking, and your body language.

Think About Your Answers

Take note that your résumé will likely set the agenda for such an interview.

More likely than not, the interviewer won't know anything about you except what's written on your résumé. This is the point where the quality of your résumé will be tested and any flaws, misunderstandings, or inconsistencies will probably come to light.

Therefore, you should prepare for any awkward questions that may possibly be raised and think carefully about the answers you're going to give so you can properly reinforce the positive impression your résumé has successfully given.

Most importantly, make sure that you can justify or expand on everything that's written on your résumé.

By being adequately prepared, you'll be better able to face any interview with the same positive attitude your résumé brings across.

To further ensure application success, here are some quick tips on preparing for your interview:

✓ Review your general knowledge.

✓ Brush up on your mathematics, as simple mathematical assessments are sometimes required.

✓ Make sure you're able to deal effectively with common customer complaints.

✓ Make sure you know what essential qualities a cabin crew should have and that you're perfectly able to demonstrate these qualities.

✓ Dress smartly in order to create the right impression.

Controlling Nerves

It's understandable for you to be nervous during interviews. After all, this phase of the recruitment process is specifically designed to assess your capabilities of working in a particular environment.

Nervousness aside, it's important for you to give the interview your best shot, which means that you need to make sure that you look and act the part. The first step to becoming a flight attendant is to look, speak, and act like a flight attendant.

How to be Prepared

Attending a job interview is indeed a daunting experience and making a good first impression will certainly help a lot. Your chances of making the kind of impression you want largely depends on how prepared you are for the interview. Do your homework and learn as much as you can about the airline.

The good news for you is that most airlines have a company website, which can be an excellent source of vital company information. Try to find out how big the company is, what their corporate values are, what major principles they stand for, and what kind of culture they have. Also try to familiarise yourself with their routes, flight schedules, and prices. Knowing the ins and outs of the company demonstrates your enthusiasm and eagerness to join their ranks.

Know What You're Getting Into

More importantly, you need to ensure that you know exactly what the job entails. An interviewer will want to be assured that you know exactly what you're getting into and that you welcome the job itself, not just the glamour that comes with it.

Thank You

You can also use email to send a thank you letter after an exploratory meeting or interview. If you do, make sure the email is sent on the same day you had your meeting or interview. If you just went through a panel interview, then make sure each panel member gets a thank you email. Many job hunters make the mistake of simply waiting for the interviewer to contact them with the result without realising that sending a thank you letter can increase their chances of getting a job offer. To make your thank you letter effective, make it simple and refer to an important detail of the interview. It's also advisable to briefly reiterate your assets at this point.

Close the letter with an appreciation of the fact that the employer took the time to interview you.

In Conclusion

Being a flight attendant crew member is considered as one of the best jobs in the world. After all, you get to travel to different places for free, live for a few days in some of the world's most popular cities, experience different cultures, taste different cuisines, and touch the lives of and hearts of travellers on a regular basis.

The lifestyle of a flight attendant is definitely one of many colours, laughter, and fun, which is why it's envied by many people. It's no wonder, then, why the selection criteria are so strict, a fact you need to bear in mind.

If you truly want to become a full-fledged flight attendant, then you need to be prepared to go through a stringent selection process as well as a rigorous training course usually lasting several months.

Here are some last tips on how to ensure success in your interview:

1. **Smile**

   This is something many candidates take for granted when they attend job interviews. They become so nervous that they end up forgetting to smile and the sad thing is that many candidates get booted out just because of this.

   Remember that a simple smile from a flight attendant can make a huge impact on a passenger's flight experience, which is why your smile is a very important consideration for the recruitment team of the world's top airlines.

   Take note as well that aviation is a very competitive industry, with thousands of individuals vying for a cabin crew post, so the simple failure to smile can indeed be enough reason for an employer to reject your application. Make sure you don't focus on the interview questions too much that you forget to flash your winning smile.

2. **Get Confident**

This is one thing all flight attendants should have and it's definitely something an interviewer will be looking for when he assesses you. Cabin crew members are responsible for the welfare of hundreds of passengers on each flight and their responsibilities include handling emergencies and talking to passengers about any number of things. It will be nearly impossible for passengers to feel comfortable in a flight with flight attendants that lack self-confidence.

3. **Show Your Personality**

This can be a little tricky, but it's important for ensuring the success of your cabin crew interview. If you can't demonstrate the kind of personality an interviewer will want to know more about, then you can kiss your chances of going through to the next round of interviews goodbye. Always remember that in a typical airline cabin crew interview, thousands of other hopefuls are waiting for you to bomb so they get a better chance at landing the job.

If you provide the usual dull answers then you'll most likely get overlooked.

If you're serious about wanting to become a flight attendant for any of the world's top airlines, then follow the guidelines here and do the best you can and you could soon be jetting off around the world.

Good luck.

13575045R00057

Printed in Great Britain
by Amazon